Experience Christmas

*preparing your heart for the manger
through the stories and songs of the season*

Christine Trevino

Experience Christmas: Preparing Your Heart for the Manger Through the Stories and Songs of the Season

Published by Amazon CreateSpace

Copyright ©2015 by Christine Trevino

ISBN-10: 1514299194
ISBN-13: 978-1514299197

All Scripture quotations, unless otherwise indicated, are taken from the Holy Bible, New International Version®, NIV®. Copyright ©1973, 1978, 1984, 2011 by Biblica, Inc.™ Used by permission of Zondervan. All rights reserved worldwide. **www.zondervan.com** The "NIV" and "New International Version" are trademarks registered in the United States Patent and Trademark Office by Biblica, Inc.™

Scripture quotations marked (NLT) are taken from the Holy Bible, New Living Translation, copyright ©1996, 2004, 2007, 2013 by Tyndale House Foundation. Used by permission of Tyndale House Publishers, Inc., Carol Stream, Illinois 60188. All rights reserved.

Any Internet addresses (websites, blogs, etc.), song titles, and corresponding artist names printed in this book are offered as a resource. They are not intended in any way to be or imply an endorsement of any kind.

All rights reserved. No part of this publication may be reproduced, stored in a retrieval system, or transmitted in any form or by any means - except for brief quotations in printed reviews - without the prior permission of the author.

Cover Art | Jacy Pulford, **www.helloawesomeshop.com**
Author Photo | Mindy Hong, **www.mishamedia.com**
Editing Services | Leah Stuhler,
   www.secretsofmommyhood.wordpress.com
Journal Font | Hans Meier, **www.fontourist.com**

For Michael, Elijah, Noah, and Micah

The four most precious jewels
in the crown of my life.

Contents

INTRODUCTION | 9

HOW TO GET THE MOST OUT OF THIS DEVOTIONAL | 13

WEEK ONE | THE STORY BEFORE CHRISTMAS | 17

Day 01 | Thin Places | 19

Day 02 | In the Beginning | 25

Day 03 | The Promise | 31

Day 04 | Silence and Waiting | 37

Day 05 | Story of a Barren Woman | 41

Day 06 | Story of a Messenger | 47

Day 07 | Light Has Come | 51

WEEK TWO | FOR BETTER, FOR WORSE | 55

Day 08 | Hard Things | 57

Day 09 | Safe Place | 63

Day 10 | Story of an Unwed Mother | 67

Day 11 | By God's Design | 71

Day 12 | Big Picture | 77

Day 13 | Story of a Carpenter | 81

Day 14 | All Things Well | 85

WEEK THREE | IN THAT TIME AND PLACE | 91

Day 15 | Welcome, Child | 93

Day 16 | Fringe Riders | 99

Day 17 | Story of an Outcast | 103

Day 18 | Peace on Earth | 107

Day 19 | Beyond the Manger | 113

Day 20 | Truth Seekers | 119

Day 21 | Rest and Listen | 125

WEEK FOUR | FOR ALL WHO WOULD COME | 129

Day 22 | Story of a Seeker | 131

Day 23 | Two Kingdoms | 135

Day 24 | Christmas Eve | 141

Day 25 | Christmas Day | 147

WHAT HAPPENS AFTER CHRISTMAS? | 151

APPENDIX | SONG LIST | 155

ACKNOWLEDGEMENTS | 159

NOTES | 161

ABOUT THE AUTHOR | 169

Introduction

It must have started when I was a child in the Christmas productions at church.

The lights. The sets. The orchestra and choir tuned and prepared, with a cast of actors ready to share the message of Christmas with a neighborhood waiting to remember.

It's what we did as a family. As a church body. From September to December, we *got ready* for Christmas. It wasn't just about putting on a show, or keeping up our creative reputation. We had something worth learning again—something worth singing about and memorizing lines for—all wrapped up in swaddling cloths, tucked away in an old wooden manger.

It's true there were other things, other memories and traditions that made the season special. But *this* one filled me with something bigger than I could explain. A kind of preparation that gave way to anticipation, and finally the celebration of Good News.

Jesus is here. Jesus is real. Jesus is *for* me, and you.

Year after year, the tradition cemented itself into my heart until *I* was writing the script, selecting songs, and directing rehearsals. That preparation continued to make my heart come alive, fresh with the hope and wonder of each new Christmas season.

It wasn't until years later, as a young wife turned stay-at-home mom trying to establish traditions for my own family, that I realized how empty it felt to come to Christmas all at once on the 24th. Trying to recreate the emotion, joy, and gratitude I knew should be there in moments of family celebration and remembrance. Feeling so terribly that something was missing. Having no idea how to recapture what I felt I had lost.

For a while, I wondered if I was just missing a beautiful piece of my history—a door God had closed without making clear what might be next. What I realized, instead, was that I was missing the long drawn-out pauses of the story; the days of preparing myself, studying Scripture, and experiencing Christmas slowly through a song, or a reading, or the response of my own heart through writing.

This all takes time.

I can still remember the Sunday we drove home from church, tears streaming down my face because I *finally* understood where the disconnect was. I *needed* the discipline of preparation—of reading and listening, writing and responding to the story God had told, long before I hit the ground running in December. At this stage of my life, I knew I couldn't go back to writing and directing like I used to. But I knew I could take a journey of remembering, giving myself space to rediscover and embrace the heart of Christmas for all that it is and all it had come to mean to me.

And so *Experience Christmas* was born.

Introduction

It was the months of writing, sifting through Christmas music, and revisiting the Biblical narrative that breathed new life into my experience of Christmas. This project helped reconnect me to the Child in the manger in an incredible way.

I hope it might do the same for you.

I'm sure I'm not the only one who gets a little busy, or a little distracted, with the demands of life at Christmas. I'm praying that God would somehow use this book to bring you closer to Him. That you would be able to slow down enough to see and feel and remember all that He has for you. And that this year you would experience Christmas like never before.

Thanks for joining me,

Christine

HOW TO GET THE MOST OUT OF THE
Experience Christmas
Devotional

I wrote this devotional with the hope of creating a daily Christmas experience that engages your heart through song, Scripture, reflection, and prayer. Devotions are divided into four weeks intended to be read every day for the first twenty-five days of December. Each day begins with a Scripture and devotional thought, followed by prompts to **Listen**, **Consider**, and **Pray**.

Listen

Included in each day's devotion is the title of a specific Christmas song that complements the day's reading. I would encourage you to google the songs on your own, or bookmark the playlist that can be found at **www.christinetrevino.com/experience-christmas-song-list/** which includes links to my favorite Christmas classics, videos uploaded by the artists, song lyrics, and iTunes affiliate links where you can purchase the music for yourself. I believe the music we hear at Christmas can be a powerful tool used to soften our hearts toward

God, preparing us for what He might choose to reveal during our time spent with Him.

Consider

The entire devotional experience points toward spiritual questions to assist you in your reflection and consideration of the day's post. It will be helpful to grab a pen to jot down your thoughts and any words God might speak to you personally through this experience.

Pray

Each post ends with a prayer prompt for your heart, your day, and your experience of Christmas. Make it personal by speaking or writing out your own prayers in a journal or in the margins of this book. I have always found the more I invest in my quiet time with the Lord, the more I am aware of how He meets me there.

"Stories of..." Vignettes

Sprinkled throughout the devotional are fictionalized vignettes highlighting some of the major players of the Christmas story. In many instances, there is no way for us to determine *exactly* what they were thinking and feeling as God wrote their story. Leaning heavily on the truth told in the Scriptural narrative, with an understanding of the social and cultural context in which these people lived, these vignettes seek to engage the reader by considering the humanity that can be found within their stories.

Mary, Joseph, Elizabeth, the shepherds, and the wise men were all *real* people, and their experience of the first Christmas unfolded in real time, much like the events of our own lives. Before these people were revered as holy characters in the divine narrative, they were ordinary people who experienced reality with honest emotions. *Just like us.*

What Happens After Christmas?

Don't let this experience end with Christmas. God wants to have a relationship with you for the other 340 days of the year as well. If you are new to faith or are interested in starting a relationship with Christ, make sure to read and implement some of the ideas in the last section of this book.

WEEK ONE
The Story Before Christmas

The story of Christmas has been told in divinely whispered promises across the pages of time. From the Garden of Eden, through Israel and her history, to the heart of a couple longing to become a family, God's promises are present and constant, extending even beyond the Scripture into the hearts and lives of His people today.

Take note of His Word. Reach your hand through the thin places this month brings, and listen for the whispers of God as He speaks to *your* heart.

DAY 01

Thin Places

*The heavens declare the glory of God;
the skies proclaim the work of his hands.*

PSALM 19:1

Then he said, "I tell you the truth, you will all see heaven open and the angels of God going up and down on the Son of Man, the one who is the stairway between heaven and earth."

JOHN 1:51 (NLT)

I absolutely believe in the idea of thin places.

There have been moments in my life where God has made Himself so real, it's as if I can feel Him standing in the room beside me. It doesn't happen often, but when it does, I am always overwhelmed by the thought that I have walked into a space where, for reasons outside my understanding, God's voice sounds clearer, and His presence infinitely more discernible than most ordinary moments of life.

> *"Heaven and earth, the Celtic saying goes, are only three feet apart, but in thin places that distance is even shorter."*

ERIC WEINER [1]

I love that the Celtics describe thin places as being spaces where heaven and earth are nearer; places where I think it becomes possible for both worlds to intersect. In my own experience, those places are almost always life-changing.

I think Christmastime is naturally one of the thinnest places of all.

If in a thin place, the divine and ordinary can meet, Christmas might be the very thinnest thin place of all. What we celebrate every year at the manger is the miracle of God becoming flesh, making His way into our world in a way we could know and understand. It's heaven meeting earth in the most beautifully practical way. There is no greater miracle, no greater gift we could ever be offered.

> *"Christmas is a thin place, a season during which even the hardest-hearted of people think about what matters, when even the most locked-up individuals loosen their grasps for just a moment, in the face of the deep beauty and hope of Christmas. The shimmer of God's presence, not always plainly visible in our world, is more visible at Christmas."*

SHAUNA NIEQUIST [2]

I believe it's possible for anyone to experience a thin place.

God doesn't make a habit of hiding Himself from us. He is active in our world and available to meet with anyone who is seeking Him. But often we get so blinded by our successes and disappointments, the things we think we know about Him, and the regular chaos of everyday life that it's possible to walk right past the invitation He extends to us.

> *"Here I am! I stand at the door and knock.*
> *If anyone hears my voice and opens the door,*
> *I will come in and eat with that person, and they with me."*

REVELATION 3:20

The challenge this month as we look toward the manger will be to make ourselves available to experience the presence of God in the middle of a wonderfully busy season, to allow space in our lives and in our hearts to recognize the thin places God has for each one of us, and maybe, *just maybe*, to ask Him to show us more clearly that He's there.

Listen

"Heaven Everywhere" | Francesca Battistelli

Consider

When was a time you experienced a thin place?

_____
_____
_____

Experience Christmas

_____
_____
_____
_____
_____

What needs to be different for you to really experience Christmas this year?

_____
_____
_____
_____
_____
_____
_____
_____

What would it look like for you to make space in your schedule to make that experience a reality?

_____
_____
_____
_____
_____
_____
_____
_____

Day 01 | Thin Places

Pray

Pray that God would give you an open heart and open mind. Commit to making space each day of Advent to fully experience Christmas this year.

Father, please show me where the thin places are. Give me an open heart and mind to hear you and receive from you. Help me to make space this month to experience Christmas in the fullest way possible.

DAY 02

In the Beginning

In the beginning was the Word, and the Word was with God, and the Word was God. He was with God in the beginning. Through him all things were made; without him nothing was made that has been made. In him was life, and that life was the light of all mankind. The light shines in the darkness, and the darkness has not overcome it.

JOHN 1:1-5

Now the serpent was more crafty than any of the wild animals the LORD God had made. He said to the woman, "Did God really say, 'You must not eat from any tree in the garden'?"

The woman said to the serpent, "We may eat fruit from the trees in the garden, but God did say, 'You must not eat fruit from the tree that is in the middle of the garden, and you must not touch it, or you will die.'"

"You will not certainly die," the serpent said to the woman. "For God knows that when you eat from it your eyes will be opened, and you will be like God, knowing good and evil."

When the woman saw that the fruit of the tree was good for food and pleasing to the eye, and also desirable for gaining wisdom, she took some and ate it.

She also gave some to her husband, who was with her, and he ate it.

GENESIS 3:1-6 [1]

In the beginning, there was God.

Holy. Omnipotent. Omniscient. Omnipresent. God.

He spoke, and there was light. Then blue sky, followed by rolling waters, and the bright green of earth. Sun, moon, and stars He hung high in the heavens, marking seasons and days and years. With a mighty filling of water, sky, and land, every creature alive in His imagination breathed deep the life of this new created world, and as His crowning work, God formed the first man and first woman.

Adam and Eve were given dominion over God's new world and the opportunity to know Him like no other created thing. God walked with Adam and Eve and called them friends. They were provided for in every way by their Father God, and given only one command: to refrain from eating the fruit of the tree of the knowledge of good and evil, because God knew it would lead to their death.

The serpent knew this too, and so he deceived Adam and Eve to follow the impulses of their hearts, disregarding the command of the Lord, their friend, changing the relationship they shared with God forever.

But God.

Holy. Omnipotent. Omniscient. Omnipresent. God.

Had already made another way.

> *"And I will put enmity between you and the woman,*
> *and between your offspring and hers;*
> *he will crush your head, and you will strike his heel."*

GENESIS 3:15

Where we inserted conflict and brokenness into our story through sin, God speaks the promise of life and reconciliation: an end to the separation we placed between us, and a future of friendship with Him.

In the moments of our deepest betrayals, God speaks promise.

God speaks life.

Because He has *always* been for us.

Listen

"God Is With Us" | Casting Crowns

Consider

In what ways do you identify with Adam and Eve?

_____
_____
_____
_____
_____
_____
_____

Where have you allowed separation in your relationship with God?

_____
_____
_____
_____
_____
_____
_____
_____
_____
_____

How has God shown you He is for you?

_____
_____
_____
_____
_____
_____
_____
_____

Day 02 | In the Beginning

Pray

Pray that God would shine the light of truth into your heart, and that you would be able to see where He is for you.

Father, thank you that you are for me; that nothing I have ever done could separate me forever from you. Thank you for making the way for me to have to a right relationship with you through your Son. Show me how to live right with you and for you.

DAY 03
The Promise

The LORD had said to Abram, "Go from your country, your people and your father's household to the land I will show you. I will make you into a great nation, and I will bless you; I will make your name great, and you will be a blessing. I will bless those who bless you, and whoever curses you I will curse; and all peoples on earth will be blessed through you."

GENESIS 12:1-3 [1]

"I will surely bless you and make your descendants as numerous as the stars in the sky and as the sand on the seashore. Your descendants will take possession of the cities of their enemies, and through your offspring all nations on earth will be blessed, because you have obeyed me."

GENESIS 22:17-18

God's promise in the garden of an end to the separation between Himself and Man was enacted by the formation and calling of a family from small beginnings. Abraham's family grew into a nation, chosen by God to embody His plans, His purposes, and His design for the entire human race.

This family, Israel, was set apart from the nations around her and given a special promise all her own—a covenant of blessing for her faithfulness and a warning of curses for her disobedience. God knew that even with the purest heart, Israel could never be perfect. In granting provision for her humanity, God created a system of sacrifice that would make right her wrongs against Him. Through this shedding of blood, Israel was offered reconciliation with God.

Over time, through generations that lost touch with both the promise and commands of God, Israel repeatedly chose her own way. She walked in the ways of the nations she was taken out of and away from the God who loved her.

But God.

Patient. Merciful. Loving. God.

Sent prophets to warn her, to remind her of the promise, and to encourage her to turn back to the ways designed by her Maker. In rebellious defiance, Israel chose to ignore these warnings and was sent away from her home into the exile exchanged for her disobedience.

Even in light of Israel's shortcomings, God did not forget His promise. Through the prophet Isaiah, He spoke of the special Holy Child that would be born to Israel.

*Therefore the Lord himself will give you a sign:
The virgin will conceive and give birth to a son,
and will call him Immanuel.*

ISAIAH 7:14

The Child God promised in the garden, conceived of unnatural means and phenomenal by supernatural proportions, was to be the Savior Immanuel.

God with us.

From Israel.

For Israel.

For to us a child is born, to us a son is given, and the government will be on his shoulders. And he will be called Wonderful Counselor, Mighty God, Everlasting Father, Prince of Peace. Of the greatness of his government and peace there will be no end. He will reign on David's throne and over his kingdom, establishing and upholding it with justice and righteousness from that time on and forever.

ISAIAH 9:6-7

Listen

"O Come, O Come Emmanuel"

Consider

What does God's faithfulness to Israel, despite her disobedience, say about His character?

_____
_____
_____
_____
_____
_____

Write down several ways God has shown His faithfulness to you.

_____
_____
_____
_____
_____
_____
_____

How has the promise of the Messiah affected your everyday life?

_____
_____
_____
_____
_____
_____

Pray

Thank God for His faithfulness to Israel, and His faithfulness to you.

Lord, thank you for being faithful, even when I am not. Thank you for making good on your promises and being the Rock I can depend on.

DAY 04

Silence and Waiting

There was a man sent from God whose name was John. He came as a witness to testify concerning that light, so that through him all might believe. He himself was not the light; he came only as a witness to the light. The true light that gives light to everyone was coming into the world.

JOHN 1:6-9 [1]

Though there is only a page turn in the Bible separating the last verse of the Old Testament with the first verse of the New, 400 years have passed for Israel in which there has been no prophet, no message, no word at all from God [2]. They are tired as a people. Dominated by Rome and spread thin across the Empire, they are hopeless with the exception of their belief in the coming of God's promised Messiah.

It is out of this silence that God speaks.

The new covenant of redemption is finally set in motion and an angel is dispatched to meet an old, weathered priest entering the temple on assignment to burn incense before the Lord.

> *"Do not be afraid, Zechariah; your prayer has been heard. Your wife Elizabeth will bear you a son, and you are to call him John. He will be a joy and delight to you, and many will rejoice because of his birth, for he will be great in the sight of the Lord."*

LUKE 1:13b-15a

I can picture Zechariah, shaking and terrified in the presence of Gabriel, now reeling from the word he's been brought. I can hear every logical fiber of his being screaming at the impossibilities, every wounded place in his heart begging not to be tempted with this kind of hope.

For years Zechariah and Elizabeth prayed for a child. He knew the stories of old. Abraham and Sarah. Isaac and Rebekah. Jacob and Rachel. Elkanah and Hannah. He knew his God could open the barren womb, and yet month after month after month, they were denied. The months turned to years, and the years brought with them the inevitable improbability that their dream of becoming a family would ever come true.

Anyone who has believed God to be miraculous, and prayed earnestly for a miracle, understands the complexities of living a life of faith while surviving the context of reality. The silence can be deafening, and the waiting demoralizing. The season filled with balanced hopes and disappointments is trying and difficult to endure.

That's why I love that God chooses to break his 400-year silence by speaking directly to the wounded heart of a barren couple. He could have chosen any way to announce to His people the promise was coming, but He chose first to whisper the promise of life into a family, and through the child born to that family, to prepare the hearts of all Israel for the Son who was coming.

Are you in a season of silence or waiting?

Remember that God is present, even when it feels like He is not, working behind the scenes of your life for His purpose and His glory.

You are never alone.

Redemption is coming.

Listen

"Winter Snow" | Chris Tomlin (feat. Audrey Assad)

Consider

Where has there been silence in your life?

_____
_____
_____
_____
_____
_____
_____
_____

What are you waiting on God for?

_____
_____
_____
_____
_____
_____

What hope and perspective can be gained from Zechariah and Elizabeth's story for your own faith journey?

_____
_____
_____
_____
_____
_____
_____

Pray

Pray that God would give you strength to remain faithful in a season of silence or waiting, and the heart to hear His voice when He speaks.

Father, I am waiting in silence this Christmas. Fill my heart with peace and my life with hope. Give me perspective to keep holding onto your promises, and speak when I need to hear you most.

DAY 05

Story of a Barren Woman

a fictionalized vignette as told from the perspective of Elizabeth

But do not forget this one thing, dear friends: With the Lord a day is like a thousand years, and a thousand years are like a day. The Lord is not slow in keeping his promise, as some understand slowness. Instead he is patient with you, not wanting anyone to perish, but everyone to come to repentance.

2 PETER 3:8-9

Both of them were righteous in the sight of God, observing all the Lord's commands and decrees blamelessly. But they were childless because Elizabeth was not able to conceive, and they were both very old.

LUKE 1:6-7

I have wanted a child of my own for such a long time. Long enough for most to think I am crazy to keep holding on to hope. Year after year, I have watched my friends hold their own babies, one after another after another, until eventually those babies had babies of their own. I try to smile and wish them well in their obvious favor, but inside I cannot often contain the heartbreak that spills over my troubled soul. I am always the one waiting; waiting with empty arms. Hoping. Praying God will turn a small measure of His favor toward me.

How long, O Lord? How long must I wait?

I am not as crazy as most think. I know that at my age I may very well go down to the grave an old and barren woman. It is this I have been most afraid of. That through all the years of praying to Almighty God, He could choose to deny me this one request; the very thing I have always believed I was created to be.

And yet I know I am not the only one who waits.

For hundreds of years my people have been met, day-in and day-out, by the silence of God. We are tired, broken from the inside out, bruised in spirit, well-worn and spent from this waiting.

How long, O Lord? How long must we wait to be redeemed?

Some have given up, casting aside the promises of Yahweh as children's tales, choosing to embrace instead the reality that is, however infuriating it may be. Perhaps for them, it is easier than allowing themselves to wonder if God hears, and if He hears, if He cares enough to do something for them.

But I cannot. Exhausted as I may be from my own life of waiting, I will hold just as tightly to the faithfulness of the God I find in Scripture, faint though His voice may be. I simply will not believe the promises of old to be any less than what they are—divinely contracted, and absolute truth.

How long, O Lord? How long until we hear from you?

As long as we have waited, I want to believe there is an answer coming, perhaps an answer I may see in my own lifetime. In my moments of quietness, stilled from the worries and questions that nag at the edges of my faith, I have hope that Almighty is moving. Strange things have happened in Jerusalem. They say my husband Zechariah has seen an angel at the temple.

If this is true, there will be a Word, and so I wait.

To be a mother.

To be redeemed.

> *After this his wife Elizabeth became pregnant and for five months remained in seclusion. "The Lord has done this for me," she said. "In these days he has shown his favor and taken away my disgrace among the people."*
>
> **LUKE 1:24-25**

Listen

"Light of the World" | Lauren Daigle

Consider

What questions or fears does a season spent waiting in silence produce in your heart?

_____
_____
_____
_____
_____
_____
_____

What truths can you hold onto in the midst of doubt?

_____
_____
_____
_____
_____
_____
_____

Where can you choose faith over fear today?

_____
_____
_____
_____
_____
_____
_____

Day 05 | Story of a Barren Woman

Pray

Pray that God would increase your faith and protect your heart from discouragement and fear.

Lord, when it is hard to hear your voice or see you moving in my circumstances, keep discouragement and fear far from me. Help me to hold onto the truths of Scripture and your promise of faithfulness.

DAY 06

Story of a Messenger

a fictionalized vignette as told from the perspective of the Angel

"And his name will be the hope of all the world."

MATTHEW 12:21 (NLT)

For thousands of years I have delivered God's messages to earth. At times His voice is gentle like the whispering wind, personal and sacred. Other times He thunders, mighty and strong, to be heard far and wide by any who would choose to listen and change. *Every* time His words are exact. True. Perfect. Life itself from the very source.

When the Maker of heaven and earth takes His moment to speak, the very ground and sky, every created plant and beast stops to breathe in the cry of their Creator. It is more wonderful, more beautiful than anything or anyone could possibly express. And this is my purpose: to humbly proclaim the messages of the King with joy and the honor of high heaven to a world waiting, longing, for His Word.

Over time He has chosen a specific group of people to speak to. Israel is His beloved among the nations and the storyteller of His plan on earth. Beginning with Abraham, Isaac, and Jacob, continuing through judges and prophets, priests and kings, the whisper of a bigger promise is spoken and heard, remembered and kept, down through time to a young girl in the little village of Nazareth.

Mary is her name.

Chosen among women, favored by God, and oh, so very blessed. The message God intended for her was *the Message* of His heart, not only for Mary, but for every person, for all of eternity. This one message generated messages to shepherds and wise men, men and women of every age and tribe and tongue for centuries to come.

This message is what heralds every other I have ever delivered: God wearing the flesh of humanity as a child.

Messiah, born to save the world.

Listen

"Messiah" | Kari Jobe

Day 06 | Story of a Messenger

Consider

Describe a time when you received a message from God.

In what ways could a messenger from God appear in your life?

What might God be speaking to you today?

Pray

Pray that you would be aware not only of God's messengers in your life, but the message He might speak to you personally.

Lord, thank you for taking interest in my life. Open my eyes to see the messengers you would send me; open my ears and my heart to the message you have for me today.

DAY 07

Light Has Come

"Arise, shine, for your light has come,
and the glory of the LORD rises upon you.
See, darkness covers the earth
and thick darkness is over the peoples,
but the LORD rises upon you
and his glory appears over you."

ISAIAH 60:1-2

The birth of Christ was never meant to be a static event, pinned to a single page of history. Our story is His story, promised by God, foreshadowed through Israel, and hopelessly longed for until God knew the timing was perfect and right to bring the Light of Christ into the world.

Jesus is the promise God made to Eve in the Garden, and the promise made to Israel.

Jesus is the promise made to Mary and Joseph, the shepherds, and wise men.

Jesus is the promise God makes to us. The one in which all our longing rests, and all the waiting of our hearts is for. He is the broken silence and the one who clears the way for us to God.

As we look forward to another week of December, let's celebrate that Light has come not only to a sin-sick world, not only to longing Israel,

But Light has come to you and me.

Listen

"Hallelujah (Light Has Come)" | BarlowGirl

Consider

In what ways does the imagery of Christ as Light in Isaiah 60:1-2 speak to you?

_____
_____
_____
_____
_____
_____
_____
_____

Day 07 | Light Has Come

Consider how the story of redemption is told through the story of Israel. What do you notice about the Christmas narrative found in the Gospels?

_____
_____
_____
_____
_____
_____
_____
_____
_____
_____

Pray

Pray that the Light of Christ would illuminate your heart and mind.

Jesus, thank you for being the Light that shines brightly through the darkness of this world and the darkness of my heart. Thank you for being present through every page-turn of history, and for coming to me in a way I could know and understand.

WEEK TWO

For Better, For Worse

Christmas can be a tender time of year when all is not right with the world. Something about this season readily exposes the cracks in our armor and the truth that we are all broken in some way or another.

When we take time to uncover the central characters of Advent, we realize they were *real* people, who faced *real* challenges, and *overcame them* with God's help. The true beauty of this season is that Christmas is a story of hope for the broken.

For better, for worse, Jesus came to meet us at the manger, brokenness and all.

DAY 08

Hard Things

This is how the birth of Jesus the Messiah came about: His mother Mary was pledged to be married to Joseph, but before they came together, she was found to be pregnant through the Holy Spirit.

MATTHEW 1:18 [1]

All it takes is two pink lines to change the entire world for first-time parents. Lifestyle. Relationships. Time. Finances. Space. *Everything* gets rearranged and reprioritized to accommodate a new life, most of all the capacity of Mom and Dad's hearts to love, believe, and dream for the future.

Being a parent is wonderfully complicated. A unique journey filled with joy and reward, it's also one of the hardest things anyone can try to do with their life.

Mary raises that admission to a completely new level.

We know little about Mary before her encounter with Gabriel, but based on the customs of her day, we can assume that she was young, probably only in her very early teens. Her engagement, whether born from love or necessity, was an expected rite of passage, and her purity during this time absolutely and unequivocally required. There would be dire consequences for a not-yet-married-but-already-pregnant young woman under Jewish social and cultural laws. [2]

But the angel said to her, "Do not be afraid, Mary; you have found favor with God. You will conceive and give birth to a son, and you are to call him Jesus."

LUKE 1:30-31

Without a doubt, Mary knows what this assignment could cost her.

This is no simple pregnancy announcement. There's no jumping-up-and-down-let's-tell-the-fam kind of excitement. Joseph could leave. Her parents could disown her. She could be *executed* for accepting the plan God has for her life. If she is fortunate enough to survive pregnancy and give birth to this Child, she knows she will likely be an outcast, unable to worship with her people. This word to Mary is heavy and serious and life-shattering in every sense of the word. [2]

"I am the Lord's servant," Mary answered.
"May your word to me be fulfilled."

LUKE 1:38a

Mary accepts her calling and the hard things that will likely follow.

God asks Mary to do an incredibly hard thing. Without the slightest hesitation Mary says *yes*. Her confidence is incredible; the capacity of her faith incomprehensible. I might have asked a few more questions, secured some hard and fast guarantees. Not Mary. She knows the voice of the Lord, and she knows the deepest desire of her heart is to serve Him.

Even if He asks her to do a very hard thing.

It's so easy for us to lose touch with the complexity of Mary's journey because we see the whole story. We know Mary, the esteemed Mother of Jesus, and forget the lonely, difficult, and entirely confusing days she lived to get there. Accepting God's call made her life incredibly meaningful, but it also made it incredibly difficult.

Sometimes God asks us to do hard things, and sometimes He asks us to live through hard things well.

So often we want the stories of our lives to be meaningful. We hope that in some way we might inspire others to live their lives well, but oh, to skip the hard things that make it that way. Oh, to avoid the hard parts at any and every cost, and to hurry them away when they are absolutely unavoidable.

A broken family? No, thank you.

A broken body? I'll pass.

A broken dream? Not me.

Hard things we are called to and hard things we must live through don't often make sense in the moment we face them, but they are the fertile soil that brings meaning and influence and depth to our lives when we choose to wear them well.

God has never been intimidated by hard things.

With His help, we don't have to be either.

Listen

"Everything Changed" | Eddie Kirkland

Consider

What hard thing is God asking you to do? What hard thing are you being called to live through well?

_____
_____
_____
_____
_____
_____
_____
_____

In what ways are you going to respond to the promptings of the Father today?

_____
_____
_____

Day 08 | Hard Things

In the middle of a hard thing, where can you put your hope for today? Tomorrow?

Pray

Pray that God would give you strength to accept the hard things He calls you to and the hard things He asks you to live through well.

Lord, I am facing a very hard thing. Bring me comfort and peace as I walk the road you have called me to. Thank you for never asking me to take on hard things without your help. Give me courage to say yes to you and the bravery I need to wear this hard thing well.

DAY 09

Safe Place

At that time Mary got ready and hurried to a town in the hill country of Judea, where she entered Zechariah's home and greeted Elizabeth. When Elizabeth heard Mary's greeting, the baby leaped in her womb, and Elizabeth was filled with the Holy Spirit. In a loud voice she exclaimed: "Blessed are you among women, and blessed is the child you will bear! ... Blessed is she who has believed that the Lord would fulfill his promises to her!"

LUKE 1:39-42, 45 [1]

Holding the secret of Messiah in her womb, Mary manages to quickly get away and find the only person she knows she can trust. Elizabeth, the barren woman turned mother-in-waiting, has also become intimately familiar with the supernatural ways of Almighty God. She too is carrying a miracle baby.

At the sound of Mary's voice, Elizabeth's child leaps inside her, and she knows Mary's secret before another word can pass between them.

> *"Blessed are you among women,*
> *and blessed is the child you will bear!"*

LUKE 1:42b

I can imagine the relief Mary feels at that moment. The secret she carries is no longer hers alone. Someone else acknowledges her story and believes it as truth. The what-ifs that lingered over Mary's heart in recent days were set to rest in the confidence of this trusted friend.

And Mary said: "My soul glorifies the Lord and my spirit rejoices in God my Savior, for he has been mindful of the humble state of his servant. From now on all generations will call me blessed, for the Mighty One has done great things for me—holy is his name."

LUKE 1:46-49

Mary is reminded in such a practical way that she will not have to walk this road alone. She is not only chosen by God to be the mother of His Son, she is seen by Him. Her fears, her questions, the longings of her heart are all known to Father God, and through the safe place provided by this precious friend, God affirms Mary in her calling.

Mary stays with Elizabeth and Zechariah for three months, long enough to be present through Elizabeth's third trimester, and even possibly at John's birth. Practically, this season is invaluable to Mary as she learns about pregnancy and childbirth through Elizabeth's experience. Spiritually, this season is even more precious because it gives Mary the time and space she needs to grow her faith for what is coming next.

This pregnancy can only be kept secret for so long.

Day 09 | Safe Place

When God calls us to do hard things or asks us to live through hard things well, He never leaves us on our own. He stands with us, sending us people who will be the spiritual and practical encouragement we need, *when we need it most.*

Listen

"Here with Us" | Joy Williams

Consider

Who has God placed in your life as a practical or spiritual encourager?

_____
_____
_____
_____
_____
_____
_____
_____
_____
_____

Where is your safe place in the Lord?

_____
_____
_____
_____
_____

What can you learn in a season that provides you with safe space to prepare your heart for hard things that may be coming?

Pray

Pray that God would show you the encouragers He has sent to you, and that He would teach you what you need to discover in that safe place in Him.

Father, thank you that you see me and know me. Thank you for being present in the seasons of difficulty and in the seasons of preparation. Show me the place of safety you have set aside for me. Show me where I can find encouragement. Teach me to become an encourager, creating safe places for others.

DAY 10

Story of an Unwed Mother

a fictionalized vignette as told from the perspective of Mary

But the angel said to her, "Do not be afraid, Mary; you have found favor with God. You will conceive and give birth to a son, and you are to call him Jesus. He will be great and will be called the Son of the Most High. The Lord God will give him the throne of his father David, and he will reign over Jacob's descendants forever; his kingdom will never end."

LUKE 1:30-33

I should be preparing for my wedding.

I should be waiting for Joseph, learning from my parents, making myself ready to become a wife. Joseph should arrive unexpectedly at our door one evening with a group of his friends to take me to the home he has been building that we'll share together. There should be singing and dancing and enough memories made with family and friends to last my whole life through. [1]

This is how it should happen.

But likely it won't. I'm pregnant . . . and it's not Joseph's baby.

It's God's.

Believe me, I know how insane it sounds. Well, either insane or blasphemous—I'm not entirely sure which one is worse—but this is the absolute truth. An angel came to me, as clear as I am speaking to you now, and told me I would become pregnant with the Son of God. If that wasn't overwhelming enough, this baby is going to be *the Messiah*. You know, the one all of Israel has been waiting on, forever.

Still, I believe what the angel said to be truth.

How could I not? Even though I have never been with a man—not even Joseph—and this belief is in something impossible and contradictory, this is my reality.

This is my destiny.

I've been praying harder than I ever have in my entire life for wisdom. I don't know what to do, or where to go, or who to talk to that would believe me, much less help me. I know the people I call friends will quickly turn into accusers the moment I begin showing. I know what they will say.

Day 10 | Story of an Unwed Mother

What they will do.

I must, at all costs, protect this Child.

The miracle I pray for now is almost greater than the first, to survive with my Child. I can only hope Joseph might stand with me, but if I must stand alone, I hold fast to the promise that God will stand beside me.

This is His Child too.

Listen

"Almost There" | Michael W. Smith (feat. Amy Grant)

Consider

How might Mary's age have affected her determination, her fear, her ability to accept the calling of God on her life?

_____
_____
_____
_____
_____
_____
_____

What causes you to question or embrace the assignment God has for you?

_____
_____
_____
_____
_____
_____
_____

What is holding you back from grasping the promises God extends to you?

_____
_____
_____
_____
_____
_____
_____
_____

Pray

Pray that God would help you let go of anything or anyone that would prevent you from becoming all He desires.

Lord, help me to lay down the expectations I have for my life in order to take up the call you have for me. Thank you that when one dream must be laid aside, you are waiting with another. Help me to dream like you do and to willingly accept what you have purposed for my life.

DAY 11

By God's Design

"For I know the plans I have for you," declares the LORD,
"plans to prosper you and not to harm you,
plans to give you a hope and a future."

JEREMIAH 29:11

This is how the birth of Jesus the Messiah came about:
His mother Mary was pledged to be married to Joseph, but before
they came together, she was found to be pregnant through the Holy
Spirit. Because Joseph her husband was faithful to the law, and yet
did not want to expose her to public disgrace, he had in mind to
divorce her quietly.

MATTHEW 1:18-19 [1]

I imagine Mary's ride back to Nazareth ending far too soon. She has spent the last three months in the safe place of Elizabeth and Zechariah's care, learning and preparing for the days ahead. She knows who she is and is confident in the life God has called her to, but on this particular day she has a very hard thing to do. Joseph, her fiancé, is still unaware of the Child that she carries, and by now she may be showing.

How do you begin this conversation with the man you're engaged to?

How do you suggest that logic and common sense no longer apply to you?

How do you explain that you are *pregnant* with the Child of *God*?

I wish we could overhear the conversation that took place between them. Joseph's shock, disbelief, anger, giving way to the pain of betrayal. Mary quiet and determined, holding tight to her faith, pleading with God to speak to Joseph in a way he could accept and understand.

Joseph is caught between the very hard place of his conviction, which demands justice, and his compassion, which begs mercy. Accepting Mary's Child assumes his role in the scandal; rejecting her would condemn her. The only way he can think to honor both conviction and compassion is to quietly divorce her.

But God.

Holy. Omnipotent. Omniscient. Omnipresent. God.

Appears to Joseph in a dream, speaks peace over his fears, and calls him to this Messianic adventure with Mary.

It was by God's design that Jesus have both mother and father to care for Him on earth. As God chose Mary, He also chose Joseph. Not by default, because of his relationship with Mary, or by merit, as if Joseph were somehow more qualified or capable than anyone else.

God chose Joseph because of his character and devotion to the Lord. As a man of conviction, discernment, and obedience, Joseph was also a servant willing to accept this very specific plan of God for his life.

A pregnant fiancée and her Child.

A future with insurmountable uncertainties.

The responsibility and headship of running a most unusual home—the home that would welcome Christ into the world.

Even when it's hard to understand.

When it is surprising and unexpected and absolutely life-changing, God still designs specific plans and purposes for lives.

Both yours and mine.

Listen

"A Strange Way to Save the World" | 4Him

Consider

Who has God called you to become?

_____

_____

_____

What is keeping you from embracing all God has for you?

What would it look like to step out in faith and confidence to embrace God's plan for your life?

Day 11 | By God's Design

Pray

Ask God to show you the plans He has for your life and to give you the confidence to walk in them.

Jesus, thank you that you have a very specific plan for my life and that your purpose for me is good. Show me how I can walk in obedience and fully embrace the life you have for me—uncertainties and all.

DAY 12

Big Picture

In those days Caesar Augustus issued a decree that a census should be taken of the entire Roman world ... And everyone went to their own town to register. So Joseph also went up from the town of Nazareth in Galilee to Judea, to Bethlehem the town of David, because he belonged to the house and line of David. He went there to register with Mary, who was pledged to be married to him and was expecting a child.

LUKE 2:1, 3-5

Stepping into their calling as expectant parents and facing their friends and family as a united front, Mary and Joseph, along with the entire Roman world were required to register for a census. Preparations were made for the nearly seventy-mile journey from Nazareth to Bethlehem in Judea, knowing it would inevitably be the birthplace of their Child.

Scripture is silent about the actual events of Mary and Joseph's travels. We don't know the exact route they took, if Mary was in her second or third trimester, or how and with whom they traveled. We don't know where they stayed when they got there, or how long they were left waiting to welcome Messiah into the world.

What we can assume with confidence is that this trip was neither convenient nor easy.

Traveling on foot or by donkey, for *any* distance, at *any* stage of pregnancy would be absolutely *horrible*. Picture Mary exhausted and swollen, every muscle screaming in protest, and Joseph watching in concern at every quiet grimace, helpless to ease her discomfort.

Still, this journey was part of God's plan.

Some 700 years prior, the prophet Micah predicted Jesus' birth in Bethlehem. Here, Mary and Joseph, moved by the hand of Rome, are making way for the fulfillment of that prophecy. [1]

> *"But you, Bethlehem Ephrathah, though you are small among the clans of Judah, out of you will come for me one who will be ruler over Israel, whose origins are from of old, from ancient times."*
>
> **MICAH 5:2 [2]**

At just the right time, God orchestrated the everyday events of history to proclaim the coming of His Son.

Centuries before, God told Israel who was coming and how He'd come, down to even the smallest of details. Christ's birth in Bethlehem is only one of many Messianic prophecies Jesus fulfills, leaving us, generations and generations from that moment in time,

Day 12 | Big Picture

with the confidence we need to believe in the truth of His coming.

These are the kind of details that cause me to marvel at the incredible lengths God took, not only to save the world, but to make space for our humanity, answering questions before we even ask them.

Listen

"O Little Town of Bethlehem"

Consider

How do faith and intellect intersect in your life?

_____
_____
_____
_____
_____
_____
_____
_____
_____

What do the fulfilled prophecies of Christ tell you about the reliability of the Christmas story?

_____
_____
_____

Experience Christmas

What does God's role in history mean for you and your story?

Pray

Pray that God would help you understand the historicity and significance of the big picture planning that led to the birth of His Son.

God, thank you for engaging my heart and mind. You have never asked me to leave my mind at the door of faith, but invite me to engage with the truth of your Word. Thank you for sending your Son to earth, and for giving me sufficient reasons to trust Him.

DAY 13

Story of a Carpenter

a fictionalized vignette as told from the perspective of Joseph

When they had gone, an angel of the Lord appeared to Joseph in a dream. "Get up," he said, "take the child and his mother and escape to Egypt. Stay there until I tell you, for Herod is going to search for the child to kill him."

MATTHEW 2:13 [1]

So much of the last several months has been about strategy and survival, moves and counter moves to keep Mary and the Baby alive. I'm used to building things with my hands—squaring off angles, hammering nails, sanding wood smooth. This new life we are living is enough to make a young man grow old very quickly.

What has been constant through the chaos is God's presence, faithful and protective. Everyone we love has their opinions and suspicions, but God has kept us from anything more, and for that we are grateful. Although the census came at the worst time of Mary's pregnancy, it did give us a sense of relief and an excuse to shield ourselves from accusing eyes. We are no one here in Bethlehem—just two faces in a crowd of many weary travelers, and the anonymity breathes a new kind of life into our tired hearts.

Except now I have discovered a new way to be lost.

The Child is here, Mary is well, and I don't know what to do with this Savior. He cries and I am helpless to understand His need. If I had thought to bring my tools at least I would have been able to make Him a crib of His own. As it is, we've taken the animal's feed trough and padded it with what we have to give him a place to sleep. He is not even here a day and already I feel like I am failing.

This is the Child of God, the Son that I have been entrusted to raise, and here he lies in a *manger*.

Mary reminds me often that God will provide, not only for our safety, but wisdom for our hearts and a lighted path for our feet. I know she is right. So while my hands are restless, I put my spirit to work, praying for His guidance.

Praying I would be enough.

Praying He will be more.

Day 13 | Story of a Carpenter

If any of you lacks wisdom, you should ask God, who gives generously to all without finding fault, and it will be given to you.

JAMES 1:5

Listen

"Word of God Speak" | MercyMe

Consider

In what areas of your life are you desperate for a word from God?

_____
_____
_____
_____
_____
_____
_____
_____
_____
_____

Where is God's wisdom most necessary for you today?

_____
_____
_____
_____
_____
_____

_____
_____
_____

What inspiration can you glean from Joseph and his role as Jesus' earthly father?

_____
_____
_____
_____
_____
_____
_____
_____

Pray

Ask God for wisdom in the areas of your life you need it most.

Father, thank you for the promise that you will grant me wisdom when I ask. Help me to ask with confidence and receive your generosity.

DAY 14

All Things Well

"Because of God's tender mercy, the morning light from heaven is about to break upon us, to give light to those who sit in darkness and in the shadow of death, and to guide us to the path of peace."

LUKE 1:78-79 (NLT)

Nestled at the end of Luke 1, between John's birth and Mary and Joseph's journey to Bethlehem, is an incredibly beautiful, poetic passage of Scripture. Zechariah has been mute since seeing the angel in the temple, and when he regains his speech he is filled with the Holy Spirit. In the most perfect recap of our study so far, he speaks a prophecy of Messiah's kingdom.

Praise the Lord God of Israel!

He is present in our midst, poised and ready to do something out-of-this-world amazing, just as He promised He would.

Yes, we have endured hard things,
but He has made a safe place for us.

*The intricate details of our lives that God has so wonderfully
orchestrated are now coming together in the master plan
He has been working on since the beginning of time.*

There is a new light dawning on us.

*Get ready.
We are about to meet the Savior.*

*All is well,
for He will make all things well.*

LUKE 1:67-79 [1] PARAPHRASE MINE

There is something catching about Zechariah's excitement, and our hearts today also resonate with the joy of this prophecy. Our Savior has come! Messiah is ours and we are given over to a new life of freedom!

All is well, for *He has made* all things well.

Even in the middle of our difficulty and distress.

When we brave the first holiday without a loved one.

When we face financial struggle, or a new normal, or the passing of a dream.

When our lives feel heavy and broken.

All can be well in our hearts, *because He came*, and because He walks so faithfully through the moments of our lives with us.

Even through the darkest nights, He is ever-present, rising as the morning star from heaven, breaking through the shadows of our hearts to bring light and illuminate peace.

Peace through the hard things.

Peace in the safe place.

Peace in your destiny.

Peace in the journey.

And that peace is something to hold onto when all is *not* well in your life.

Christ came to show us the way to peace. As we look toward another week of study, let us cling to the promise that all is well in our hearts and in our soul, *because Christ has come*, and His coming gives us the hope that makes it so.

Listen

"All Is Well" | Michael W. Smith (feat. Carrie Underwood)

Consider

What are you struggling with this Christmas?

_____

_____

Where do you need God's peace in your life?

How can things be well in your heart, independent of what is or is not well in your world?

Pray

Invite God into your story and into your struggle. Ask Him to give you the peace that passes all understanding in your situation.

Jesus, thank you that I can have hope in you, despite what is or is not well in my life. Father, lead me in the path of peace, and help me to cling to you through the changing moments of my life.

WEEK THREE

In That Time and Place

Recorded alongside the birth of Christ are the responses of His contemporaries. In heaven and on earth, from family to fringe riders, prophets, and kings, the visitors to the manger were many and varied. Within their stories we find an open invitation for everyone, from the least to the greatest and with every variance between, to come and bow at the manger today.

DAY 15

Welcome, Child

While they were there, the time came for the baby to be born, and she gave birth to her firstborn, a son. She wrapped him in cloths and placed him in a manger, because there was no guest room available for them.

LUKE 2:6-7

The grand stage of God's plan is set with the major players ready and in place. Mary is in the final days of her pregnancy, and with Joseph, they have arrived at the prophesied birthplace of Messiah. The world is moments away from welcoming the Son of God.

One might expect the unveiling of God's plan of redemption to be heralded by parades and celebrations throughout the earth, with royalty and celebrity, intellectuals and influential leaders of every kind called to lend their welcome to the King of all Kings. Surely the celebration of this promised Child would be nothing less than grand and glorious and unforgettable.

But God.

Holy. Omnipotent. Omniscient. Omnipresent. God.

Chose a different kind of welcome.

His Child will be ushered into a city overcrowded with census travelers, busy about their own affairs. The two He called as parents are unable to secure their own room and end their journey in the company of lowly animals. Mary labors as any other woman, struggling to breathe through contractions and the pain they send radiating through her body. Joseph, an unlikely midwife, assists Mary in the ways she cannot help herself. Likely, this birth is messy and long, punctuated by the open-air cries of a newborn babe, who is hushed and swaddled in the only cradle available—a rough feed trough called a manger. [1]

Nothing grand or glorious, and at first glance, seemingly forgettable.

God's Son is welcomed by a simple man and his young wife, scared, tired, and beside themselves with joy at the flesh and bones of God's answered promise.

It is no mistake that the culminating promise of the ages comes to us in the form of a fragile child—God wearing skin so we could see Him and touch Him. He could have appeared to us all-powerful and all present, clothed in the glory of heaven.

But then how could we gather the confidence to approach Him?

How could we identify with a God so beyond our world of understanding?

Day 15 | Welcome, Child

The miracle of His gift cracks our hearts open wide to embrace a new way of meeting God.

A baby, we understand. A baby, we are drawn to. A baby, invites us to come as we are, with what we have, no questions asked, no expectations made.

Jesus set aside the glories of heaven for a season, limiting and defining Himself in words we could understand. That's why this gospel is so marvelous, so scandalous. No one has ever reached a hand into humanity like Christ, to meet us where we are, to grasp us for eternity.

No one has ever gone to such great lengths to save us, but God.

Listen

"Welcome to our World" | Chris Rice

Consider

What do you think it was like at the manger? Describe how you picture Christ's birth.

_____
_____
_____
_____
_____

How does Christ's humanity and divinity play into your understanding of the Christmas story?

How does Christ's entrance into our world speak to you personally?

Day 15 | Welcome, Child

Pray

Pray that God would open your heart to wonder at the enormity of this gift and understand what His place in your life should be.

Jesus, thank you for limiting yourself in such an amazing way to reach me. Thank you for speaking to me in words I can understand, and for loving me enough to come to my rescue.

DAY 16

Fringe Riders

That night there were shepherds staying in the fields nearby, guarding their flocks of sheep.

LUKE 2:8 (NLT) [1]

Jesus is finally here.

While Mary and Joseph quietly revel in the miracle of this new Child, God begins spreading the Good News of His promised Son's arrival.

In an instant, a group of shepherds guarding their flocks of sheep outside of Bethlehem are terrifyingly stunned by the awesome presence of a messenger from God.

Don't be afraid! I have good news—the Savior, God's promised Messiah has been born.

The angel tells them where to find the Baby and how they will recognize Him, and in the blink of an eye, one angel becomes the whole host of heaven splashed across the sky, praising God in loud and confident voices:

> *"Glory to God in the highest,*
> *and on earth peace, good will toward men!"*

LUKE 2:14 (KJV) [2]

This is the type of welcome we would expect to herald the birth of the King of Kings.

Yet this announcement, bold and supernatural, is significant in another very subtle, very important way. There is no royalty in the fields outside of Bethlehem. The high priest and religious leaders are likely going about a normal evening completely oblivious to God's appointment with humanity. Anyone with any kind of platform or influence is noticeably absent, strikingly unaware of this most blessed and holy event.

Shepherds were the lowest of persons, nearly invisible to the people around them. They had few rights, little influence, and even less significance in the society in which they lived. [3]

This people group, riding on the fringe of acceptable society, are the ones God reveals His Son to *first*.

> *The shepherds said to each other, "Let's go to Bethlehem! Let's see this thing that has happened, which the Lord has told us about."*

LUKE 2:15 (NLT)

Day 16 | Fringe Riders

These shepherds are validated by the God who sees beyond their status and situation. They are the privileged few who hear God's announcement firsthand, and then become the first messengers of His glad tidings to the world.

How blessed are we that Christ did not only come in a way we could see Him and know Him, but He came for *all* of us, even those of us who find ourselves riding the fringe.

Listen

"Angels We Have Heard on High"

Consider

What truths from the story of the shepherds can you absorb into your everyday actions?

_____
_____
_____
_____
_____
_____
_____
_____
_____
_____

Experience Christmas

How do you think God sees fringe riders today?

_____
_____
_____
_____
_____
_____
_____
_____

Pray

Pray that God would make you aware and sensitive to His heart for fringe riders today.

Jesus, thank you that you came for everyone—the marginalized, the left-out, the fringe riders. Make me aware of your heart for the world and the value you place on each person created in your image.

DAY 17

Story of an Outcast

a fictionalized vignette as told from the perspective of a shepherd

But the LORD said to Samuel, "Don't judge by his appearance or height, for I have rejected him. The LORD doesn't see things the way you see them. People judge by outward appearance, but the LORD looks at the heart."

1 SAMUEL 16:7 (NLT)

All my life I have been invisible.

As my father has been, and my grandfather, and his father before that. We are shepherds. Nameless, faceless, would-be thieves to our countrymen, and avoided at any and all costs.

It is true I've met my share of shepherds who live up to everyone's underwhelming expectations, but to say we are all despicable and untrustworthy is as ridiculous as saying every priest is hypocritical and power hungry (although at times I do wonder).

It's so challenging to sort through the truth and the lies (what with us being such ignorant sinners and all). Funny how priests and worshippers both know how to find us when there is a sacrifice to be made. Then and only then is it acceptable to speak to a shepherd.

I may not be allowed into the synagogue, and God Himself help me if I step foot inside the temple, but I have read the Scriptures for myself (shocking as it may be to speak with a literate shepherd). Many of my friends don't want anything to do with God. I can't blame them for the way His people treat them, but I've always felt it was my unquestioned duty to rebel against the system—if even in such a tiny, private way. This is what I have discovered—

I don't think God is like *any* of them.

Over and over again He uses shepherds for His work. Abraham, Issac, and Jacob. Moses. King David. The prophet Amos. He even likens *Himself* to a shepherd.

God says there is something inside of *me* that's like *Him*.

The thought is so radical even I have a hard time believing it. But it's there, plain as day spread throughout the Scriptures. I have come to wonder if people secretly cut these passages out. It must make them so angry, but *these* are the parts that really make me smile.

The events of last night make me certain my suspicions about God are correct. An angel appeared to us late in the fields, singing about good news from God. His Son's been born to a young girl and a carpenter in Bethlehem. He is wrapped up in strips of cloth, lying in a manger.

The Messiah is here, and we have seen Him.

Listen

"O Holy Night"

Consider

What words would you use to describe yourself?

_____
_____
_____
_____
_____
_____
_____
_____

What words do you think God uses to describe you?

_____
_____
_____

In a world obsessed with youth and health and beauty, in what ways can you assume a Godly perspective of the people around you?

Pray

Thank God that He sees beyond the physical to examine our hearts.

Lord, thank you for looking beyond my cultural perspectives and outward appearance to see who I really am inside. Help me to acknowledge your image inside of me and your image in those around me. Help me to see others as you do.

DAY 18

Peace on Earth

"Glory to God in the highest, and on earth peace, good will toward men!"

LUKE 2:14 (KJV) [1]

These are the very words the angels proclaimed the night that Christ was born, speaking promise and life into a world waiting for the hope of Messiah.

And yet what do they speak to our world today?

In a world torn apart by genocide and wars, where children go hungry, and human beings are bought and sold, *where is the peace*? Where is the hope? How can we reconcile the declaration of the angels with our sin-sick, heartbroken world?

> *And in despair I bowed my head:*
> *"There is no peace on earth," I said,*
> *"For hate is strong and mocks the song*

Experience Christmas

Of peace on earth, good will to men."

HENRY WADSWORTH LONGFELLOW [2]

This question of pain and suffering is not one that answers easily. Theologians and persons of faith have been engaging it for years, but this question is so crucial to our experience of Christmas that it cannot be ignored. [3]

What I have come to understand through study and the wrestling of my own heart is the following:

God respects us so much as beings created in His image that He allows us to have and exercise our own will. For good or for evil.

God could have made us like puppets, with His hand pulling every string of our lives. But without the freedom to choose for ourselves, there would be no real love, or joy, or life. God took an incredible risk allowing us to choose our own way. This risk is the very essence of our humanity, separating us from every other created thing on earth. It is a gift endowed to us by our Creator.

God is not only aware of the pain and suffering in this world, He is present and broken over the things that break us.

*The LORD is close to the brokenhearted
and saves those who are crushed in spirit.*

PSALM 34:18

God does not delight in the folly of our choices. It breaks His heart when people are abused, ignored, and rejected. It is He who walks with us through the darkest black of night, and He who will wipe every tear of sorrow from our eyes. We are not forgotten by the God who loves us through our suffering.

You keep track of all my sorrows.
You have collected all my tears in your bottle.
You have recorded each one in your book.

PSALM 56:8 (NLT)

Christ's birth is the peace God extends to a wounded world.

When the angels sang peace on earth, they were not announcing the end of free-will. They were proclaiming God's entrance into our chaos, bringing peace into our midst through Christ.

The God present at humanity's fall in the Garden of Eden is the God present with us at the manger. He is the Child Immanuel, God with us. He is Calvary's Savior come to make right our relationship with Him. He is the King-Coming-Soon who will someday replace the brokenness of this world with a new heaven and a new earth, perfect and wonderful and whole.

Christ is our peace now, walking with us through the storms of life.

He is the peace that makes it possible for us to know God.

He is the peace that secures our destiny in heaven.

He is the peace that will make our world right someday.

As recipients of God's peace, we are called to be His peace-bearers to the world today.

> *No, O people, the LORD has told you what is good,*
> *and this is what he requires of you:*
> *to do what is right, to love mercy,*
> *and to walk humbly with your God.*
>
> **MICAH 6:8 (NLT)**

God invites us to be His arm extended to a wounded and dying world—to see injustice and pain, to acknowledge the poor and afflicted, to allow our hearts to break with the things that break His, and then *to do something about it in His name.*

> *Then pealed the bells more loud and deep:*
> *"God is not dead, nor doth he sleep;*
> *The wrong shall fail, the right prevail,*
> *With peace on earth, good will to men."*
>
> **HENRY WADSWORTH LONGFELLOW [2]**

This is what the angels proclaimed.

And this is why we can believe the truth of their message.

Christ is the peace that's come to earth, God's offering of goodwill toward us.

Day 18 | Peace on Earth

Listen

"I Heard the Bells on Christmas Day"

Consider

What have you discovered by reflecting on the message of peace the angels proclaimed?

As a recipient of God's peace, how might you be a maker of peace in your world?

Pray

Ask God to show you how He is working to bring peace on earth and ask Him to soften your heart toward the broken and hurting in your life.

Father, thank you that Jesus is the peace offered to me here on earth. Help me to hold onto that promise when I see the broken places of my heart and the broken places of my world.

Lord, I ask that you would bring peace where there is unrest in our world and peace where evil still reigns. Jesus, bring peace to my heart and teach me to discern where I can be a peace-bearer in the world.

DAY 19

Beyond the Manger

When the time came for the purification rites required by the Law of Moses, Joseph and Mary took him to Jerusalem to present him to the Lord ... and to offer a sacrifice in keeping with what is said in the Law of the Lord.

LUKE 2:22 & 24a [1]

Like any new parent, Mary and Joseph have begun to settle into something that resembles a routine with their newborn son. Nearing forty-days as a family, they make preparations for a journey to Jerusalem where they will present Jesus to the Lord, as was the custom of their people.

While the excitement of the angels and shepherds have subsided, the wonders of this Child do not cease to amaze Mary and Joseph. Standing in the comings and goings of the bustling temple courts, they are singled out by a godly man Simeon, who recognizes their Child for who He really is.

Messiah.

I can almost hear Simeon gasp with knowing, extending his hand to touch Jesus, a hesitant Mary looking to Joseph for reassurance. This stranger, asking for their baby, knows only what God could have told him, and so Jesus passes from mother to prophet.

Simeon holds the Child, perhaps with tears streaming down his face, and marvels at the faithfulness of God. Perhaps Mary and Joseph share a smile of knowing; the heavy beating of their hearts confirming to them that God is present in this meeting.

Simeon looks from Child to parents and speaks a word of blessing over them. He then locks eyes with Mary and prophesies:

> *"This child is destined to cause the falling and rising of many in Israel, and to be a sign that will be spoken against, so that the thoughts of many hearts will be revealed. And a sword will pierce your own soul too."*

LUKE 2:34b-35

Mary's breath catches.

*A sword will pierce **my** soul?*

Why? How? What do you mean?

Frantically she scans her memory for anything she can connect to the initial message of the angel.

> *The Lord God will give him the throne of his ancestor David. And He will reign over Israel forever; his Kingdom will never end.*

LUKE 1:32b-33 (NLT)

The angel said nothing about a sword to her soul, but before she can ask Simeon what he might mean, they are greeted by another divinely informed visitor. The prophetess Anna exclaims with excitement at the sight of God's Son and begins telling the people around them about the promised Child now present in their midst.

The questions in Mary's heart are never voiced in the excitement at the temple.

We don't know how Mary processed this word from Simeon, but I am certain it stuck fast in her heart. With the supernatural all over the life she's become accustomed to, this word could not have been taken lightly. Mary's been given the first glimpse of life beyond the manger for herself, for her Son, and I wonder if it's what she had expected.

When you read through the Gospels of Jesus' life and ministry beyond the manger, He is often misunderstood by the people who think they know who Messiah will be, what He will do, and how He will change the world. In the society that He was born, to the people He was born to, there is an expectation that Messiah will come to free them from the power Rome holds over their lives.

But Jesus' purpose was so much bigger than Israel, and so much greater than Rome.

Here, within the first weeks of His arrival, Mary is already warned that her life, and her Son's, will not progress according to her expectations.

A Savior, not like the Savior they expected.

Jesus came to the manger to walk toward the cross.

> *Surely He took up our pain and bore our suffering, yet we considered him punished by God, stricken by him, and afflicted. But he was pierced for our transgressions, he was crushed for our iniquities; the punishment that brought us peace was on him, and by his wounds we are healed.*

ISAIAH 53:4-5

Listen

"Mary Did You Know?"

Consider

What kind of Savior have you expected Christ to be?

_____
_____
_____
_____
_____
_____
_____
_____

Day 19 | Beyond the Manger

How do your expectations of Christ line up with the truth of what we find in the Bible?

_____
_____
_____
_____
_____
_____
_____
_____
_____
_____

Pray

Pray that God would reveal to you the truth of Christ's coming and His purpose in your life.

Jesus, help me to lay aside what I think I know of you, and what I expect from you, to come to you with a heart hungry to know who you really are and what you want to do in my life. Thank you that your purpose extends beyond the manger. Help me to grasp the enormity of your story for me, and in me.

DAY 20

Truth Seekers

*"I see him, but not now;
I behold him, but not near.
A star will come out of Jacob;
A scepter will rise out of Israel."*

NUMBERS 24:17a [1]

In Luke 2:21-38, we witnessed the interaction between Mary, Joseph, Simeon, and Anna at the temple, possibly leading to Mary's first glimpse of life for them beyond the manger. While Luke 2:39-40 describes Jesus going straight from the temple to Nazareth, many scholars agree it is more likely Mary and Joseph traveled with him back to Bethlehem, where the chronology of our story is picked up at the beginning of Matthew chapter two. [2]

It is here that we are introduced to the Magi, a group of wise, learned men who have spent time studying Scripture, watching the skies for signs of the promised King to be born to Israel. Tradition has inserted all kinds of theories about these travelers, but Scripture gives little detail of their journey, and even less about the company of travelers that arrived in Jerusalem from the East that day. [3]

What we do know for certain about this group of truth seekers is that they are hungry for an encounter with Messiah.

Picture opulent figures with flowing, exquisite robes riding into the city. Without an air of indifference or importance, one dismounts and hurriedly asks the nearest local where he and his party can find the new King.

Blank stare. *I'm sorry, do you mean Herod?*

The wise man shakes his head. *This fellow must be confused.*

He approaches another, and another, and another, and it seems *no one* knows about the birth of this new King. More Magi dismount to tether their animals and begin questioning the people.

> *"Where is the newborn king of the Jews? We saw his star as it rose, and we have come to worship him."*
>
> **MATTHEW 2:2 (NLT)**

The city is shockingly unaware, incapable of helping these foreign strangers, but the idea of a new king is something they can get behind. When the question of the Magi finally reaches Herod's palace, he is terrified what the answer may mean for his reign. In a panic he reacts, quickly bringing the priests and teachers of religious law together to discern from the Scriptures what might be going on.

Where is this Messiah supposed to be born? Herod thunders.

Bethlehem, they tell him. *The Messiah is supposed to be born in Bethlehem.*

Herod steadies his breathing as a plan begins to form in his mind. He invites the Magi in for a private meeting, confidently entertaining their questions, and sends them onward to Bethlehem with the instructions to bring news of this new Child back to him.

So that I too may go and worship him.

It matters why we come to the manger.

People are motivated to search after God for all kinds of reasons, and I think at times, it is those reasons that have much to do with our encounter of Him.

We see this so plainly played out in today's portion of the Christmas narrative. As Matthew continues, we find that the truth-seeking Magi did, in fact, find Jesus in Bethlehem and worshiped Him, as they desired. Herod, motivated by fear, his lust for power, and the tyranny of his own will, did not.

God *always* reveals Himself to truth seekers.

In Psalm 139 it says that God knows us inside and out. He knows when we sit and when we rise, when we come and when we go. He knows us in the fullest way we can possibly be known.

For this reason we can hold tight to the most impossible hope. When we are honestly and actively seeking the truth of who He is, there is no other logical end to our story, *than to find Him.*

Listen

"The First Noel"

Consider

What is motivating your search for the Christ Child this Christmas?

_____
_____
_____
_____
_____
_____
_____
_____

What do you hope to encounter at the manger?

_____
_____
_____
_____
_____
_____
_____
_____

Day 20 | Truth Seekers

How is your faith journey impacted by the knowledge that God reveals Himself to truth seekers?

Pray

Pray that God would guide your search for Jesus this Christmas, and that He would open your heart to the revelation of His truth.

God, thank you that you never turn away an honest truth seeker. Thank you for guiding the steps of my spiritual journey to the place that I can find you and experience the joy and peace that comes from living life with you. Be with those in my life who are searching right now. Lead them, guide them, and help them find what they are looking for in you.

DAY 21

Rest and Listen

But the Lord said to her, "My dear Martha, you are worried and upset over all these details! There is only one thing worth being concerned about. Mary has discovered it, and it will not be taken away from her."

LUKE 10:41-42 (NLT)

I am so in awe of the God we serve.

Who sent us a Savior we could know and understand.

Who seeks out the less-than, the marginalized, the fringe riders, and entrusts them with promise and purpose.

Who extends His only Son to us as an offering of goodwill and the promise of peace in our broken and hurting world.

Who saw beyond the manger to the cross that would redeem us and forever seal us as His own.

And yet, I am so prone to miss the whispers of His love.

Beyond the noise of our lives, there are angels still singing, and thin places taut with closeness. Christmas is coming. We have each been on a journey this month—waiting, preparing, exercising our longing for the promised Messiah—and the celebration is near.

As we look toward the final days before Christmas, let's make space to clear our hearts of the clutter, and quiet the noise around us. Let's rest from the hurry and the doing of Christmas to listen, *really* listen, to the song that's being sung.

O ye beneath life's crushing load,
Whose forms are bending low,
Who toil along the climbing way
With painful steps and slow;
Look now, for glad and golden hours
Come swiftly on the wing;
Oh rest beside the weary road
And hear the angels sing.

EDMUND HAMILTON SEARS [1]

Listen

"It Came Upon a Midnight Clear"

Day 21 | Rest and Listen

Consider

What *good things* are crowding out the space in your life reserved for remembering the *best thing* this Christmas?

_____
_____
_____
_____
_____
_____
_____
_____
_____

What might need to be reprioritized, added to, or deleted from your final Christmas celebration to-do list?

_____
_____
_____
_____
_____
_____
_____
_____
_____

What do you need to do to prepare your heart in the coming days for Christmas?

_____
_____

Pray

Pray that God would help you find the space you need to rest, listen, and prepare yourself for Christmas.

Father, thank you for your love. Thank you for wanting the very best for me and the very best of me. In the middle of what could be stressful days leading up to family celebrations, help me to rest and listen, to hold onto what matters, and to keep my eyes firmly fixed on you.

WEEK FOUR

For All Who Would Come

The ultimate gift of Christmas is a personal one, and therefore our response must be as well. How will we approach the manger? What do we bring to this promised Child-King? How will we remember the Savior, not only at Christmas, but throughout the story of our lives?

These are some of the most important questions we can ask ourselves—questions that often take time and space to consider. Christmas is so much more than just a few moments of December spent with friends and family.

It has the potential to transform our very lives.

DAY 22

Story of a Seeker

a fictionalized vignette as told from the perspective of a wise man

For God, who said, "Let light shine out of darkness," made his light shine in our hearts to give us the light of the knowledge of God's glory displayed in the face of Christ.

2 CORINTHIANS 4:6

Some people spend their lives searching for wealth, or recognition, or achievement. Others search for beauty, meaning, love. I have spent mine searching the Scriptures for whispers of the promised Jewish Messiah, and the skies for the star that will herald His birth. [1]

The more I learn, the more I am consumed with the pursuit of this King.

There is no doubt He will be great, carrying on the dynasty of His father David, and a wonderful counselor to His people. He is to be a Savior and Redeemer of Israel—the manifestation of God Himself with us in our humanity. A promise of Light that extends even to the heart of the Gentile.

But for all that I know, there is still so much that perplexes me.

If the Scriptures are correct, as I am inclined to believe they are, it appears He will endure much hardship. The betrayal of a friend. The unexplained hatred of His peers. Beaten and striped for the very people He loves. Prophecy for prophecy, it seems His calling will cost Him His very life.

How is it He will be both exalted and persecuted? Loved and rejected? What kind of Child, what kind of Messiah is it we are waiting for?

The answer may come more quickly than I know.

There has been movement in the heavens. A star that must signal His coming. And so there are some making themselves ready, preparing gifts with the hope they will be presented to this long-awaited Child-King.

I too will be on this journey to Jerusalem. I don't know what answers might be found in Him still so tender in His mother's care, but I must go. If only to see Him with my eyes, and bow my knee in worship.

This is my life.

This is my prayer.

Day 22 | Story of a Seeker

Listen

"What Child Is This?"

Consider

How would you describe your spiritual journey?

_____
_____
_____
_____
_____
_____
_____
_____
_____
_____

What are you spending your life searching for?

_____
_____
_____
_____
_____
_____
_____
_____
_____
_____

What do you hope your life's search finds?

_____
_____
_____
_____
_____
_____
_____
_____

Pray

Ask God to guide the searching of your heart toward Him.

Lord, illuminate the darkness of my heart with your light. Keep my life focused on the things that really matter and help me to understand who you really are.

DAY 23

Two Kingdoms

After they had heard the king, they went on their way, and the star they had seen when it rose went ahead of them until it stopped over the place where the child was. When they saw the star, they were overjoyed. On coming to the house, they saw the child with his mother Mary, and they bowed down and worshiped him. Then they opened their treasures and presented him with gifts of gold, frankincense and myrrh.

MATTHEW 2:9-11 [1]

The Magi leave Jerusalem with Herod's blessing to pursue the Child, and that night they find again the brilliant star in the sky that started them on their journey. It led them through the quiet streets of Bethlehem right to Mary and Joseph's home, where they get their very first glimpse of Jesus.

All the nights of searching and waiting, longing and hoping, fulfilled in an instant with one look at God's promise made flesh.

One by one they approach, bowing to the ground before the King in worship. Each Magi in turn approaches with a gift meant to honor Him: gold fit for the King of all Kings, frankincense for the Priest who would stand between God and Man, and myrrh for the Savior who would die in our place.

I can see Mary overwhelmed by this outpouring of love for her Son, God's Son, tucking away this moment deep in her mother's heart, willing it to last forever.

They see. They know. They understand.

This Child, God's promise and plan, this Light that broke through the shadows of her own heart has now pierced the darkness in another, as light is always meant to do.

Having completed their journey, filled to the full of God's goodness, the Magi are warned in a dream not to return to Herod but to travel home a different way. Herod, eventually learning of their betrayal, sends orders to kill all the little boys in Bethlehem, hoping to extinguish the Light.

But God.

Holy. Omniscient. Omnipotent. Omnipresent. God.

Had already warned Joseph in a dream to escape to Egypt until the time was right to bring them back home to Nazareth.

Until the time was right to share this Light with the whole world.

There are always two kingdoms at odds at the manger.

Day 23 | Two Kingdoms

Like the Magi, like Herod, it is impossible to come to the manger and leave unmoved or indifferent. There is either a falling-down-to-worship experience or the defense of your own kingdom.

Your life.

Your family.

Your money.

Your time.

Your way.

Or God's.

When you really experience Christmas, when you truly understand the Savior and the lengths He took to win your heart, you understand there is a choice you have to make.

And only you can make it.

> *O come, let us adore Him,*
> *O come, let us adore Him,*
> *O come, let us adore Him,*
> *Christ the Lord.*

JOHN WADE [2]

Listen

"Adore Him" | **Kari Jobe**

Consider

What in your life shows evidence of the Kingdom you are living for?

What would surrendering to the Kingdom of God look like for you?

How can you "come and adore" Jesus this Christmas?

Day 23 | Two Kingdoms

_____
_____
_____
_____

Pray

Ask God to shine a light into the current condition of your heart and ask Him what the next steps of your faith journey should look like.

Search my heart, Lord. Help me to surrender the parts of my life that I try to hold back from you. Help me to come to you in the spirit of the Magi, worshipping with abandon and giving my very best. God help me to meet you at the manger and adore.

DAY 24

Christmas Eve

The Word became flesh and made his dwelling among us. We have seen his glory, the glory of the one and only Son, who came from the Father, full of grace and truth.

JOHN 1:14 [1]

Growing up we always celebrated Christmas Eve with my dad's parents.

Before the stockings and presents and everything a child could wish for on Christmas Day, there was Oma and Opa's house, and the quiet of Christmas Eve.

Oma and Opa were simple people, German immigrants who left their family and home for a new life in America before my dad was born. Christmas Eve at their house kept that simplicity close. Instead of a traditional tree trimmed and centered in the picture window, red poinsettias, candles, and fresh evergreen branches decorated their table. Gifts leaned heavily toward predictability and practicality—a bag of pfeffernusse cookies, a bar of marzipan, and an envelope of cash slipped to my parents for our college fund. We ate fresh chicken from the coop with mashed potatoes and gravy and plates of vegetables I always passed over. For dessert we had Oma's homemade fruit tarts and streuselkuchen, and drank lemon-lime soda with juice for as long as we could get away with.

At some point after dinner, Opa would feel his way to the living room and lower himself to the old wooden chair by the television set to find his violin case. My entire life Opa was blind. Still, every Christmas, as if to beckon everyone away from the chatter and the dishes, he brought out his violin, tuned it to his pitch pipe, and began playing his favorite carol.

> *Silent night, Holy night*
> *All is calm, all is bright*
> *Round yon virgin, mother and child*
> *Holy infant, so tender and mild*
> *Sleep in heavenly peace,*
> *Sleep in heavenly peace.*

JOSEPH MOHR [2]

Slowly, the background noise would fade. Everyone would make their way into the room, while he'd sway in time to the music, and we'd sing—some in English, some in German. When Opa pulled his bow across the string for the last note, there was a beat of silence before my dad or my uncle would pray a prayer of thanksgiving for the year we'd been able to share, and a blessing for the year that was to come.

I was so young, only thirteen the last time we shared a Christmas together like that. I didn't fully understand the significance of that family moment, except that this was what we did on Christmas Eve before bundling up to attend service on our way home.

Now I see what a gift it was that Opa gave to us.

A moment in one of the best and busiest times of year to pause and reflect.

To feel with our ears and our hearts and our voices.

And to look closely for one last thin place of the season.

I've never been able to listen to "Silent Night" without that certain feeling of reverence carried over from the Christmas Eves spent at my grandparents' house. And like my Opa beckoning us away from the kitchen with his violin, it beckons me to stop and consider what holiness we celebrate at Christ's birth.

How He changed the world.

How He changed me—

With His coming.

What matters most today is that we take time to wonder at the manger.

To give ourselves space to find the thin place.

To let the Light flood into our hearts.

To listen and feel and be drawn in by the miracle we've been given.

And then to share it by the life that we live.

Listen

"Silent Night"

Consider

What Christmas Eve traditions do you (or your family) have that honor the Savior?

_____
_____
_____
_____
_____
_____
_____
_____

What tradition could you start new this year?

_____
_____
_____
_____
_____
_____
_____
_____

Day 24 | Christmas Eve

How will you wonder at the manger today?

_____
_____
_____
_____
_____
_____
_____
_____
_____
_____

Pray

Thank God for the gift that Jesus is to you personally.

Lord, thank you for the miracle that came to earth over two thousand years ago as a Baby in a manger. Thank you that Jesus came to rescue me and to offer me real and full life. Warm me with your presence, and help me to celebrate you with an undivided heart today.

DAY 25

Christmas Day

The true light that gives light to everyone was coming into the world. He was in the world, and though the world was made through him, the world did not recognize him. He came to that which was his own, but his own did not receive him. Yet to all who did receive him, to those who believed in his name, he gave the right to become children of God – children born not of natural descent, nor of human decision or a husband's will, but born of God.

JOHN 1:9-13 [1]

Merry Christmas!

I hope that today is not only filled with the joy of friends and family but also with the fullness of God's presence in your life.

I hope that you have found the space you've needed to wonder at the miracle of Christmas and that you are ready and prepared to fully experience this day like no other Christmas Day before.

I pray that something through this journey has awakened your heart, tugging you closer toward the Savior.

We *all* need a Savior.

This is the fundamental truth at the very heart of Christmas. Not one of us is capable of standing before God, pure and perfect and free of sin on our own. Like Adam and Eve, our sin has separated us from God forever, and that sin condemns us to death.

But Jesus.

Sweet Jesus has made the way that leads to life with God. Born to us at Christmas, He lived the perfect life we could not and carried our sin to the cross where He became death for us, making us right with God.

When we admit that we are sinners in need of rescue,

When we acknowledge that Jesus is the Christ, God's promised Savior and Redeemer,

When we believe that He died for us, rising again three days later, victorious over our condition,

When we confess that He is Lord of our lives,

We. Can. Be. Saved.

This is the gift that came to us as a baby in the manger.

This is the promise of God fulfilled and complete.

This is the honest-to-goodness real and vibrant life we have been searching for, bringing with it the most joyous hope we could ever know.

Peace with God.

And *this*, friends, is why we celebrate the miracle of today.

Listen

"What Love Is This" | Kari Jobe

Consider

Have you accepted the gift of Jesus? Are you confident of your right standing with God through Him?

_____
_____
_____
_____
_____
_____
_____

What next steps might God be asking you to take in your spiritual journey?

_____

How will your experience of Christmas this year affect your life moving forward?

Pray

Thank God for His gift of salvation through Jesus Christ, and by faith, accept it.

Jesus, I know that I am a sinner in need of your grace. I know that your sacrifice on the cross exchanged the death I deserved for new life in your name. I ask that you would forgive me. By faith I trust in you for my salvation and acknowledge you as the Lord of my life.

What Happens After Christmas?

Christmas is really just the beginning.

Like Christ's birth into humanity was the beginning of God's plan unfolding on earth, perhaps this Christmas has become the beginning of God's plan unfolding in your life and in your heart.

If you have never before accepted the gift of salvation and the promise of new life in Christ, I would encourage you to do that today. The book of Romans has a lot to say about how to start a relationship with Christ:

1. The Bible is very clear that each and every one of us is a sinner who stands condemned before a pure and holy God (Romans 3:23, 3:10-18).

2. In Romans 6:23, it says that the wages of our sin is death, but that Jesus is the gift of God who brings us life (Romans 5:8).

3. When we confess Jesus as Lord of our life, believing that He was

crucified in our place, and raised to life from death, the Bible says that we can be saved (Romans 10:9).

4. God doesn't show favoritism. All who accept this gift by faith can expect to freely receive it (Romans 10:13).

5. Placing our faith in Christ, we can experience true peace with God, both here and for all eternity (Romans 5:1, 8:1, 8:38-39) [1].

Salvation is also a beginning.

True and meaningful relationships are cultivated over time, and the same principles apply to a growing relationship with Christ. Here are three practical ways to commit to your spiritual growth:

Take time to read the Word of God.

If you're new to the Bible, start with the book of John. If you don't have a Bible, YouVersion is a great free Bible app that also supports devotional reading plans.

Talk to God daily.

You don't have to be in a certain place or posture, with all the right words written out in front of you, to pray. Just talk to God. Let Him into your everyday needs, concerns, and joys. In Ephesians 6:18 it says to pray on all occasions with all kinds of prayers and requests. Your Father loves to hear your voice, and as you're listening, you'll begin to discern His.

Find a group of like-minded believers.

Life with Christ was never meant to be lived alone. Find a church body that you can share with, learn from, and walk through this life with Jesus together.

Faith is meant to be a lifelong journey.

The life of faith does not come with a promised guarantee of ease, security, or prosperity. Sometimes life can be unexplainably difficult. Even for people who choose to follow Jesus.

> *"Be strong and courageous. Do not be afraid;*
> *do not be discouraged, for the LORD your God*
> *will be with you wherever you go."*
>
> **JOSHUA 1:9**

What we *are* promised is that we will never walk alone. We can live life confidently and boldly with the knowledge that wherever we go, whatever we do, whatever struggles we may face in life, we are walking with the God who holds the entire world in His hand.

The God who raised Christ from death into life.

The God who takes such interest in our lives that He would do whatever it took to rescue us from ourselves.

This is the greatest joy we can glean from Christmas, and the greatest story we can live with our lives.

The experience of peace with God.

APPENDIX

Song List

This entire list of songs, including links to my favorite renditions of Christmas classics, videos uploaded by artists, lyrics, and iTunes affiliate links can be found online at **www.christinetrevino.com/experience-christmas-song-list/** or by scanning the QR code at left with your phone or mobile device.

WEEK ONE

"Heaven Everywhere" | Francesca Battistelli

"God Is With Us" | Casting Crowns

"O Come, O Come Emmanuel"

"Winter Snow" | Chris Tomlin (feat. Audrey Assad)

"Light of the World" | Lauren Daigle

"Messiah" | Kari Jobe

"Hallelujah (Light Has Come)" | BarlowGirl

WEEK TWO

"Everything Changed" | Eddie Kirkland

"Here with Us" | Joy Williams

"Almost There" | Michael W. Smith (feat. Amy Grant)

"A Strange Way to Save the World" | 4Him

"O Little Town of Bethlehem"

"Word of God Speak" | MercyMe

"All Is Well" | Michael W. Smith (feat. Carrie Underwood)

WEEK THREE

"Welcome to our World" | Chris Rice

"Angels We Have Heard on High"

"O Holy Night"

"I Heard the Bells on Christmas Day"

"Mary, Did You Know?"

"The First Noel"

"It Came Upon A Midnight Clear"

Appendix | Song List

WEEK FOUR

"What Child Is This?"

"Adore Him" | Kari Jobe

"Silent Night"

"What Love Is This" | Kari Jobe

Acknowledgements

Readers, thank you for supporting the work I do on my blog. Thank you for picking up this book, for reading, engaging, and sharing with others. You make doing what I love possible.

There are three congregations that have played an influential role in my spiritual journey, where seeds of the dream of this book were planted, watered, and grown. I am so grateful that Northwest Assembly of God, Soul City Church, and Willow Creek North Shore have been part of my story.

Thank you to my editor and friend Leah Stuhler, for putting the final touches on the final manuscript, to all the people who helped me figure out licensing concerns for this project, and for the friends and family who helped me get the word out about *Experience Christmas*.

Kristal Arnold, Katie Payne, and my husband Mike, THANK YOU for reading an early draft of the manuscript and for your incredibly amazing feedback. This project was taken to a whole new level because of your input. Your support, encouragement, and ability to talk me off of creative ledges, have meant the absolute world to me.

Mom and Dad, you taught me to believe that I could do absolutely anything. Thank you for believing the same.

Elijah, Noah, and Micah, where would I be without the three of you?

You have brought meaning to my life in ways I never expected. Thank you for sharing me with this project. I'm so glad God chose me to be your momma.

Michael, I wrote my first script at your request almost fifteen years ago not knowing how writing would turn into such a passion and eventually bring us together. Thank you for seeing God at work in my life and calling out the best in me. You have always, always, *always* believed I could do this. I'm so glad you picked me.

Finally, and most importantly, thank you, Jesus. Your faithfulness to me is amazingly unmerited and your grace so wonderfully overwhelming. Over and over again you patiently teach me what it means to walk with you.

There is truly no other journey I'd rather be on.

Notes

Day 01 | Thin Places

1. Weiner, Eric. "Where Heaven and Earth Come Closer." *Travel | Cultured Traveler*. The New York Times, 9 March 2012. Web. 11 Nov. 2014
   Quote printed with the permission of the author.

2. Niequist, Shauna. *Bittersweet: Thoughts on Change, Grace and Learning the Hard Way.* Grand Rapids: Zondervan, 2010. Print.
   Quote printed with the permission of the author.

Day 02 | In the Beginning

1. For more of the story, see the Biblical account of Creation and the Fall as recorded in Genesis 1-3.

Day 03 | The Promise

1. For more of the story, see the Biblical account of Abraham's life as recorded in Genesis 12-25.

Day 04 | Silence and Waiting

1. For more of the story, see the Biblical account of Zechariah and Elizabeth as recorded in Luke 1:5-25 and 1:57-80.

2. "What Were the 400 Years of Silence?" *gotQuestions.org*. n.p. n.d. Web. 18 April 2015.

Day 08 | Hard Things

1. For more of the story, see the Biblical account of Mary and the angel as recorded in Luke 1:26-38.

2. Fairchild, Mary. "Mary - Mother of Jesus, Humble Servant of God." *About Religion*. n.d. Web. 11 Nov. 2014.

Day 09 | Safe Place

1. For more of the story, see the Biblical account of Mary and Elizabeth as recorded in Luke 1:39-66.

Day 10 | Story of an Unwed Mother

1. The Archdiocese of Washington published an article on their blog entitled "What were weddings like in Jesus' day?" that provides a valuable description of what Jewish weddings would have been like at that time in history.

Day 11 | By God's Design

1. For more of the story, see the Biblical account of Joseph as recorded in Matthew 1:18-25.

Day 12 | Big Picture

1. There is so much that has been written on the historicity of Jesus and His fulfillment of Old Testament prophecies. The following resources were helpful to me, and may be helpful to you as well:

    a. Fairchild, Mary. "44 Prophecies Jesus Fulfilled." *About Religion*. n.d. Web. 11 Nov. 2014.

    b. Arch, Dave. "Old Testament Prophecies Fulfilled in Jesus' Life." *AskAPastor.org*. 2002. Web. 11 Nov. 2014.

    c. *The Case for Christ: A Journalist's Personal Investigation of the Evidence for Jesus*. Lee Strobel.

2. For the entire Biblical prophecy, see Micah 5:2-4.

Day 13 | Story of a Carpenter

1. I firmly believe Joseph was a praying man. While Scripture is silent about him during Jesus' later years, he certainly played a key role in Christ's infancy. Not only is he told of Mary's immaculate conception in Matthew 1:18-25, he is warned in a dream to flee to Egypt in Matthew 2:13-18, and then given two sets of instructions for their return to Israel in Matthew 2:19-23. Joseph was a man who followed God's instructions for his

family immediately and completely.

Day 14 | All Things Well

1. For Zechariah's entire prophecy, see Luke 1:67-79.

Day 15 | Welcome, Child

1. I found the following articles fascinating resources on what historians and theologians believe it may have been like at the manger:

    a. McKnight, Scot. "Book Excerpt: The Real Mary." *The Christian Broadcasting Network.* n.d. Web. 11 Nov. 2014.

    b. Taylor, Paul S. "What are the most common misconceptions about Jesus Christ's birth?" *ChristianAnswers.net.* n.d. Web. 27 Apr. 2015.

    c. "Was Jesus born in a stable?" *ChristianAnswers.net.* n.p. n.d. Web. 11 Nov. 2014.

Day 16 | Fringe Riders

1. To read the Shepherds entire story, see Luke 2:8-20.

2. King James Version. (Public Domain).

3. Alcorn, Randy. "Shepherds Status." *Eternal Perspectives Ministries.* 11 Mar. 2008. Web. 11 Nov. 2014.

Day 18 | Peace on Earth

1. King James Version. (Public Domain).

2. Longfellow, Henry Wadsworth. "I Heard the Bells on Christmas Day." (Public Domain).

3. One of the most exceptional explanations I have ever come across on the subject of pain and suffering is from a message by Bill Hybels (founding pastor of Willow Creek Community Church) entitled *Why?* This would be an incredible resource to watch for anyone in the process of discerning the answer for themselves personally.

Day 19 | Beyond the Manger

1. For more of the story, see the Biblical account of Simeon and Anna as recorded in Luke 2:21-38.

Day 20 | Truth Seekers

1. For more of the story, see the Biblical account of the wise men and Herod as recorded in Matthew 2:1-8.

2. Chaffey, Tim, and Bodie Hodge. "Christmas Timeline of the Biblical Account." *AnswersInGenesis.org*. 21 Dec. 2010. Web. 27 Apr. 2015.

3. Chaffey, Tim. "We Three Kings: Clearing up Misconceptions." *AnswersInGenesis.org*. 14 Dec. 2010. Web. 27 Apr. 2015.

Day 21 | Rest and Listen

1. Sears, Edward Hamilton. "It Came Upon a Midnight Clear." (Public Domain).

Day 22 | Story of a Seeker

1. Arch, Dave. "Old Testament Prophecies Fulfilled in Jesus' Life." AskAPastor.org. 2002. Web. 11 Nov. 2014.

Day 23 | Two Kingdoms

1. For the entire story of the wise men and Herod, see Matthew 2:9-23.

2. Wade, John Francis. "O Come All Ye Faithful." (Public Domain).

Day 24 | Christmas Eve

1. The Gospel of John presents Jesus as the Word of God present from the very beginning of time. See John 1:1-18 for an incredible summary of Christ's role at creation, His purpose in coming, and the hope we can have because He did.

2. Mohr, Joseph. "Silent Night." (Public Domain).

Notes

Day 25 | Christmas Day

1. See John 1:1-18 for John's summary of Christ's role at creation, His purpose in coming, and the hope we can have because He did.

What Happens After Christmas?

1. The following resources were helpful in outlining Scripture references from Romans for this chapter, and will be extremely helpful should you choose to make a decision for Christ today.

    a. "What is the Romans Road to Salvation?" *gotQuestions.org*. n.p. n.d. Web. 15 May 2015.

    b. "The ABCs of Salvation." LifeWay Church Resources. n.p. n.d. Web. 15 May 2015.

About the Author

Christine Trevino holds a Bachelor of Arts in Ministerial Studies from Christian Life College. Previously, she served as a staff pastor in administrative and creative arts, and in various departments of the Assemblies of God state headquarters in southern Illinois. In 2009, Christine and her family returned to the Chicagoland area so her husband could go back to school, and she could become a stay-at-home mom to their infant son.

Motherhood, in a very literal sense, turned her life inside out and shone a light of discovery on some of the true passions of her heart. Fast-forward two kids later, Christine now homeschools her oldest boys, and works from home as a freelance writer, blogger, and author. A large portion of the scripts she has written for church drama presentations can be found online for free at her self-titled blog **www.christinetrevino.com**, where you can also find her chatting about faith, family, and creativity regularly.

Christine is passionate about the power creative arts can have in the Church and in the hearts of individuals to bring them closer to Christ. She hopes this book might be one of those tools in your life.